Th CHRISTMAS SPIRIT:

Let Peace and Joy

Fill your Heart

Brian Morgan (signature)

Brian Morgan

This book is associated with the website www.brianmorganbooks.com.

A Kindle eBook version of this book is available, as are eBooks in other formats (see the website).

Printed by CreateSpace for the publisher and available online through Amazon.com.

ISBN-13: 978—1493708291

ISBN-10: 1493708295

The author gratefully acknowledges that this book could not have been published without the hard work, advice and loving support of his wife of 50 years, Judy Morgan.

Contents

"We hear the beating of wings over Bethlehem and a light that is not of the sun or of the stars shines in the midnight sky.

Let the beauty of the story take away all narrowness, all thought of formal creeds.

Let it be remembered as a story that has happened again and again, to people of many different races, that has been expressed through many religions, that has been called by many different names.

Time and space and language lay no limitations upon human brotherhood."

The New York Times (25 December 1937)

Introduction

What is it about Christmas? What is it that makes the world pause and hearts open up and peace and goodwill abound?

Some say it's magic. Some call it a mystery that doesn't really need to be solved, just enjoyed. We all tend to call it simply the *Christmas Spirit*. And it's different for each one of us.

Religion is behind it, of course, but why is it that people around the world of different religions really love Christmas?

There are simply no words to tell you what I feel at Christmas, but I really want to show you glimpses of that Christmas Spirit.

I hope and believe that, although our lives may be different, the same heart beats within each one of us and the same feelings swamp our lives at this time of the year.

What started it for me? Well…

Once upon a Christmas time, long ago, when I was about six, I was at a neighbour's home while my mother was in hospital. I was playing in the back yard and I think I caught my first tadpole (or some such momentous event). I raced up the path and burst in through the door to show my "Aunty Jean". It was a moment to shape a lifetime.

There, on the couch, sat my "aunt" with her new-born son at her breast. I was absolutely stunned. I had never seen anything like this before. She made no attempt to cover up, but just smiled and quietly asked me to wait outside. I still remember her serenity.

I think I did as she asked, but this was the most beautiful thing I had ever seen. Things like this were never talked about in those days, but, instantly, I knew what was going on. I knew she was feeding the baby. I understood with the sudden clarity of an epiphany.

In that instant, I realised that this woman, and all women, were very special. They actually gave birth to babies and, wow, nurtured them. The awe I felt then for women has never left me, nearly seven decades later.

And the baby boy… The new-born baby scent remained the most beautiful smell in my memory, until my own children were born.

I don't know when the insight came to me, whether it was immediate or crept up just because it was Christmas, but this baby made me change the way I thought of the other baby, born 2000 years before, and nurtured in a stable.

Until that day, when I burst in on a mother and her baby, I had thought of Christmas as just a time for gifts and fun. But that mother and baby changed my feelings at Christmas for a lifetime. Everything was suddenly different.

A few days later, as I shuffled up the aisle of the church to see the nativity set, the mother and baby figures might as well have been real flesh and blood. (And, as you'll see later in the *Silent Night* story, my feelings about that baby were shared by Father Joseph Mohr).

Yes, Christmas was never the same again. This year, as in every year, scenes from Christmases Past crowd my memory and the Christmas Spirit is alive again.

It can come upon you anywhere, anytime. Suddenly that Christmas feeling will fill you with love, with joy, with happiness, with that deep feeling of tranquillity and peace.

For me, it once came as I wandered into the living room in pre-dawn darkness and found the Christmas tree in the shadows. Little baubles tried to glisten in the pale light. The house was silent and there were few presents, as was usual in those days (and still is usual for many), but, in that stillness, I was suddenly swamped with the serenity only Christmas brings.

I do love that breathless anticipation as first light gradually wakes the children and their sounds of joy wake the adults. I'm in my 70s as I write this, but I always love to be "the first kid in the street awake" on Christmas morning.

The Christmas Spirit can simply come because it's the time of giving. The story of the Three Wise Men started it, and each of us try to follow the tradition by finding gifts for those we love. And the gift if not as important as the thought behind it. Don't we just love the gifts that children and friends make for us with their own hands, their own skills?

The spirit can come with the voice of a friend, the hug of a loved one, the smiles, the laughter, the food (if you are fortunate), the jabbering voices, the sanctity of the church or chapel or holy place.

It can come drifting in on the sounds of Christmas – the carols, the hymns, the voices lifted heavenward and bursting with the Christmas Spirit.

It can come simply because love is in the air and because peace and goodwill to all can be so infectious. Troubles and differences and pain and sorrow can be forgotten for this brief, beautiful time of giving and sharing.

I'm afraid I'm overwhelmed right now just thinking about it, so I'll stop the preamble and start the stories and share the thoughts of Christmas.

Illustration for The Legend of the Christmas Prayer *by Sergio Martínez.*

I'll share what others have thought over the years, but, for my part, the first story, *The Legend of the Christmas Scrolls*, is a rebirth of "a classic little gem of a book" that became a sell-out bestseller in the US, the UK and Japan, when a version of it first appeared some years ago as *The Legend of the Christmas Prayer*. So many people have asked to see it published again. It's about giving when you have nothing to give.

The second story, *The Greatest Gift*, is a short one about the real and beautiful things we can give each other, and, again, money is not necessary.

The third story, *Silent Night: The True Story of a Christmas Miracle*, is bound to touch a chord with those who love Christmas carols.

For now, please accept these thoughts and stories, and may they spark in you the same feelings of happiness and love I feel right now.

That is my fervent wish for you this Christmas and every Christmas.

Brian Morgan

The Legend

of the

Christmas

Scrolls:

The Story of the

Twelve Wishes

Brian Morgan

Once upon a Christmas time,

long ago,

a man who had a big heart,

but little money,

dreamt he could give his friends

endless riches.

When he awoke,

the dream kept running

through his mind,

over and over.

Finally, he asked himself:

"If I could give my friends anything,

what would I give?"

He smiled

as he began to think

of all the wondrous things

he could buy for them.

But then he thought:

"I'm a happy man,

yet I have none of those things."

And he began to think
that perhaps real wealth
could not be measured
in riches.

Perhaps there were gifts
of greater value
than the things
money could buy.

In the still of the night,

he pondered these things

and thought of Christmas

and what it meant to him.

Taking out his quill,

he began to write

on parchment scrolls:

On the first day

of Christmas,

I wish you joy in abundance

and laughter,

for laughter cures our ills

and joy makes

the spirits soar.

On the second day

of Christmas,

I wish you a sigh

when you need one,

for a sigh clears the heart

as a cough clears the throat,

and with a sigh

comes acceptance of

what we cannot change.

On the third day

of Christmas,

I wish you tears

when you need them,

for tears clear the eyes

to see the stars

and cleanse the soul

to let healing begin.

On the fourth day

of Christmas,

I wish you serenity,

for fights and wars

start in individual breasts

and that is where

they must end.

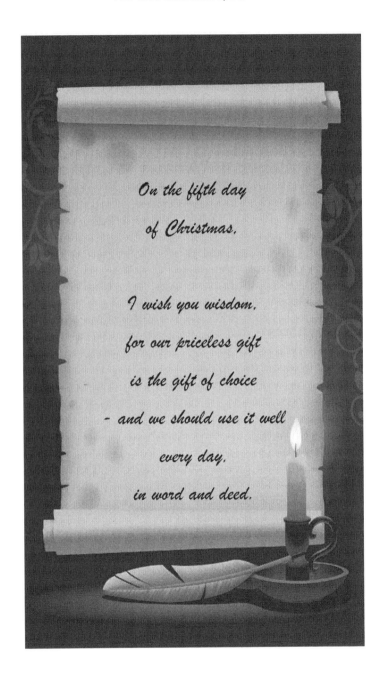

On the fifth day

of Christmas,

I wish you wisdom,

for our priceless gift

is the gift of choice

- and we should use it well

every day,

in word and deed.

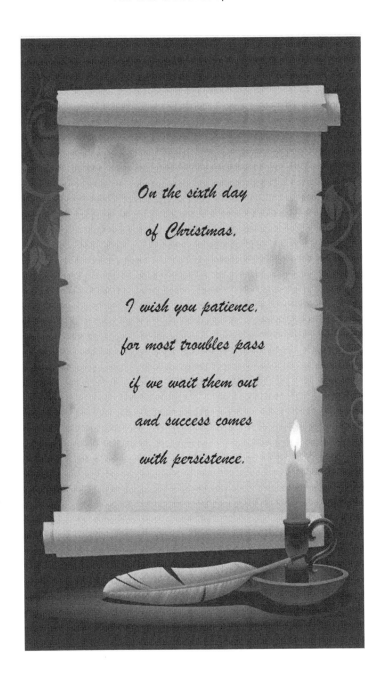

On the sixth day

of Christmas,

I wish you patience,

for most troubles pass

if we wait them out

and success comes

with persistence.

On the seventh day

of Christmas,

I wish you courage,

for there may be many

pitfalls and dangers ahead

and problems can only be solved

when they are faced.

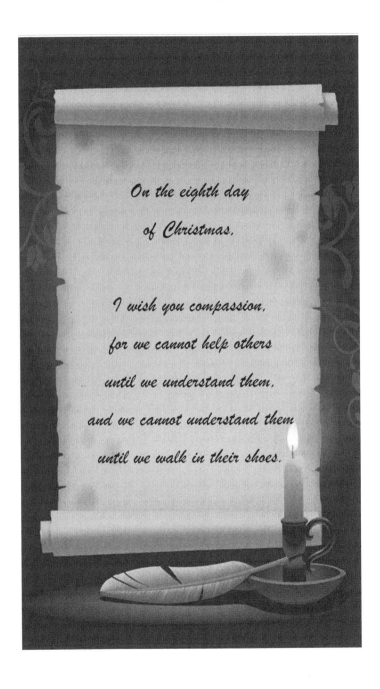

On the eighth day

of Christmas,

I wish you compassion,

for we cannot help others

until we understand them,

and we cannot understand them

until we walk in their shoes.

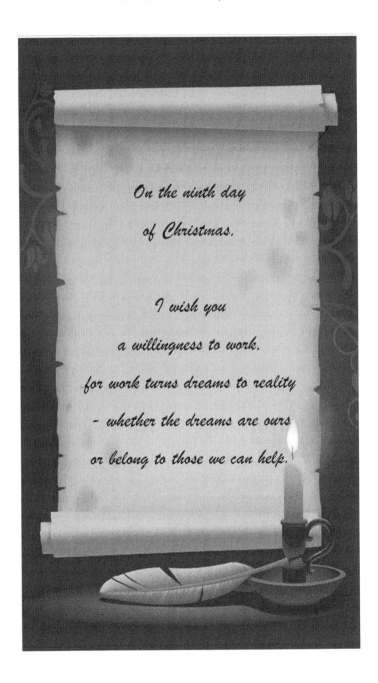

On the ninth day

of Christmas,

I wish you

a willingness to work,

for work turns dreams to reality

- whether the dreams are ours

or belong to those we can help.

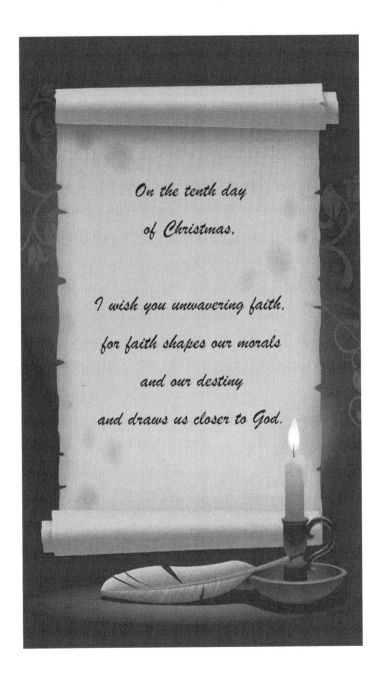

On the tenth day
of Christmas,

I wish you unwavering faith,
for faith shapes our morals
and our destiny
and draws us closer to God.

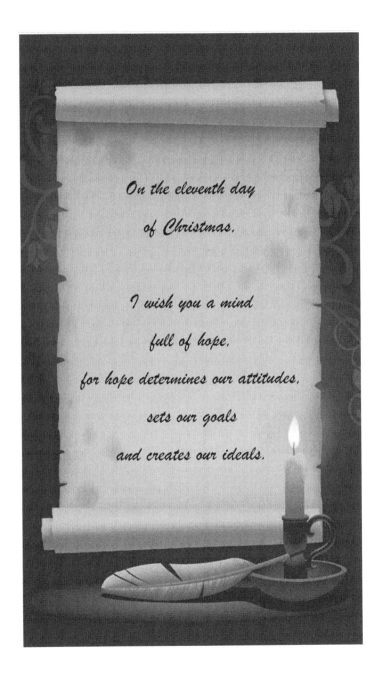

On the eleventh day

of Christmas,

I wish you a mind

full of hope,

for hope determines our attitudes,

sets our goals

and creates our ideals.

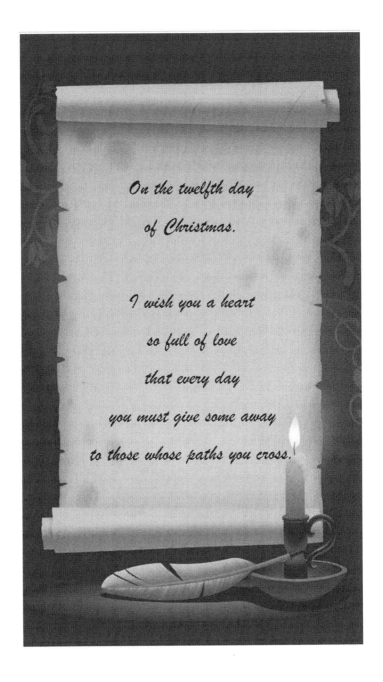

On the twelfth day
of Christmas,

I wish you a heart
so full of love
that every day
you must give some away
to those whose paths you cross.

And, with each wish,

and with each scroll,

the man realised he was not

giving a gift at all,

but wishing that his friends

would discover the gifts

they already had within them.

Each time he wrote a wish,

a magical thing happened.

It seemed to him that the wish,

although offered to his friends,

remained in his heart,

and produced in him

the very thing he wished for them.

The man copied his scrolls

and sent the

Twelve Wishes of Christmas

to special friends

and that is where the legend

of the Christmas scrolls was lost

in the mists of time.

The man quietly slipped into oblivion,

but, over the years,

the Twelve Wishes of Christmas

began to appear again

all over the world,

and the legend began a life without end.

People in obscure villages and big cities
would receive at Christmas time
a copy of the scrolls from a friend.

Every year, those who had copies
would dust them off
and quietly read them on
Christmas Eve, and remember.

On Christmas morning, more people
would find the legend under their trees,
and so the magic multiplied,
until the story
finally reached you.

But, along the way,
as Christmas approached one year,
an old man, alone,
walked the streets of the city,
watching the bustle
and enjoying the festive decorations.

He didn't have much,
but he had time on his hands.
His friends were all gone,
but he had
his memories.

Memories of people, of places,

of Christmases past,

of the peace and serenity

only Christmas can bring.

As he strolled, a lit-up shop window

caught his eye;

a display of small books.

He leaned closer

and read the title

through eyes

dim with years:

The Legend of the

Christmas Scrolls

He rubbed his eyes

and looked again.

Could this be?

Could this really be?

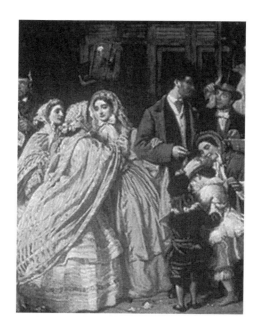

He shuffled into the shop
and picked up a book
with trembling hands.

He flicked through the pages
and a smile
began to wrinkle his eyes.

The old man didn't need
to read the words;
they were exactly
as he had written them
all those years ago
for his friends.

The friends were now gone,
but the words ... the words remained.

As he held the book,

the years slipped away.

He remembered the feelings he had

when he first put

quill to parchment

and offered those friends

his gifts of the heart.

When the old man left the shop,

his back was a little straighter;

his step a little lighter.

There was a little

something in his eyes

as he greeted those he met.

Tomorrow would be

the First day of Christmas ...

... and already he felt,

deep within,

a surge of joy...

joy in abundance.

And, for the first time

in a long, long time,

he felt the urge to laugh.

And his spirits soared.

The Original

Christmas

Story

According to
Luke and Matthew

The birth of Jesus, according to Luke

And it came to pass in those days that a decree went out from Caesar Augustus that all the world should be registered. This census first took place while Quirinius was governing Syria.

So all went to be registered, everyone to his own city.

Joseph also went up from Galilee, out of the city of Nazareth, into Judea to the city of David, which is called Bethlehem, because he was of the house and lineage of David, to be registered with Mary, his betrothed wife, who was with child.

So it was, that while they were there, the days were completed for her to be delivered.

And she brought her first-born Son, and wrapped Him in swaddling cloths, and laid Him in a manger, because there was no room for them in the inn.

Now there were in the same country shepherds living out in the fields, keeping watch over their flock by night.

And behold, an angel of the Lord stood before them, and the glory of the Lord shone around them, and they were greatly afraid.

Then the angel said to them:

"Do not be afraid, for behold, I bring you good tidings of great joy which will be to all people.

"For there is born to you this day, in the city of David, a Saviour, who is Christ the Lord.

"And this will be the sign to you: you will find a Babe wrapped in swaddling cloths lying in a manger."

And suddenly there was with the angel a multitude of the heavenly host praising God and saying:

"Glory to God in the highest,

"And on earth peace, goodwill to all men."

So it was, when the angels had gone away from them into heaven, that the shepherds said to one another, "Let us now go to Bethlehem and see this thing that has come to pass, which the Lord has made known to us."

And they came with haste and found Mary, and Joseph, and the Babe lying in a manger.

Now when they had seen Him, they made widely known the saying which was told them concerning this Child.

And all those who heard it marvelled at those things which were told them by the shepherds.

But Mary kept all these things and pondered them in her heart.

The Wise Men and Herod, according to Matthew

Now after Jesus was born in Bethlehem of Judea in the days of Herod the King, behold, wise men from the East came to Jerusalem, saying, "Where is He who has been born King of the Jews? For we have seen His star in the east and have come to worship Him."

When Herod the King heard this, he was troubled, and all Jerusalem with him.

And when he had gathered all the chief priests and scribes of the people together, he inquired of them where the Christ was to be born.

So they said to him, "In Bethlehem of Judea, for thus it is written by the prophet:

> *"But you, Bethlehem, in the land of Judea,*
> *Are not the least among the rulers of Judah;*
> *For out of you shall come a Ruler*
> *Who will shepherd my people Israel."*

Then Herod, when he had secretly called the wise men, determined from them what time the star appeared.

And he sent them to Bethlehem and said, "Go and search carefully for the young Child, and when you have found Him, bring back word to me, that I may come and worship Him also."

When they heard the king, they departed; and behold the star which they had seen in the east went before them until it came and stood over where the young Child was. When they saw the star, they rejoiced with exceedingly great joy.

And when they had come into the house, they saw the young Child with Mary His mother, and fell down and worshiped Him. And when they had opened their treasures they presented gifts to Him: gold, frankincense, and myrrh.

Then, being divinely warned in a dream that they should not return to Herod, they departed for their country another way. ■

The Greatest Gift:

It's the gift we all crave

Brian Morgan

The Greatest Gift is the gift we all can give, and the gift we most want to receive. It is something we can all afford, no matter how poor we are. And, when we give this treasure away, we keep it, and it continues to grow.

Once upon a time of Christmas giving, not so long ago, there lived a man who was very poor. He was a good man, with a heart of gold, who worked hard to provide for his family, but never seemed to have many coins to lavish gifts upon them.

He was a simple man, a fact that worried him from time to time. Every so often it occurred to him that he was not achieving a great deal with his life.

He wondered what he could do to make his life more worthwhile. He thought he should be able to leave the world a better place than he found it.

He felt he should have some purpose, some reason for being. However, it was a quandary he could not resolve and, as usual, he turned to work to set his mind at ease.

On this Christmas Eve, he worked quietly in his workshop, fashioning some playthings from wood and painting old toys to make them new again. He wanted, with all his heart, to have gifts for his family, even if he had no coins.

The man took an old, much-loved doll and began to restore its charms, so that it could be loved again. And as he carefully painted the doll's smile, he smiled.

He thought of his daughter's laughter and her arms around his neck and her lips recoiling at the tickle of his whiskers.

What can a poor man give such a beautiful child?

"I will give you the things you already have," he thought. "I will give you the virtues that are already, by instinct, within you waiting to bloom. In a thousand ways you will not even notice, I will nourish the virtues of courage and wisdom and understanding and fortitude and love.

"I will do this simply by giving you all that is within me of these things, as my parents gave them to me. And those virtues will blossom within you, and you will blossom.

"A man cannot live for his children," he thought. "He can only show them how to live."

And, as he worked with his hands, he smiled to himself. He thought of his little son. Such a joy the boy was as he sat on his father's shoulders or grasped his hand.

"My son," he thought, "I will always give you a hand, in ways you will never realise. A hand to heal, a hand to mend, a hand to support, a hand just to hold."

The man looked at the dusty picture of the Praying Hands on his workshop wall. "I will give you my prayers," he thought, "not just in the season of giving, but every day.

"I will do more than that," he thought, as he began to realise the real gifts he could give his son.

"I will make sure I have time on my hands to give you. I will give you the time to grow strong in knowledge and wisdom and confidence, so that you can face the world without me.

"Until you realise that you must be you, you might want to be like me. I will therefore always strive to be honourable and worthy of imitation.

"I will give you the best I can give. I will give you everything I can of me – everything you need until you no longer need me."

What else can a poor man give?

His hand shook a little as he thought of all he had to give his children. He smiled at the thought that he could give without them even knowing what they were receiving, until, one day, perhaps, they would realise how much they truly had.

He set the toys aside so that his wife could wrap them with ribbons and bows and magic. And, as he did so, his thoughts turned to the woman he loved more than words could say – the one who was his partner, his special friend, his lifetime companion.

"What can I possibly give you? I cannot give you fine clothes, or jewellery, or expensive perfumes. One day, perhaps, but what can I give you when I am poor?" he thought.

"How can I give you the things you deserve when I have nothing?

"What would you wish for," he mused, "if you could have just one wish this Christmas time?"

He smiled at the very thought of the question and tried to think as she would think. He did not have to think for long. He knew.

If she could have just one wish for Christmas, she would not want beautiful things for herself or fine things for the home – or even expensive gifts for her family.

If there was just one wish, it would just be to love and be loved. That is all.

"Ah yes," thought the man, "that is just what she would wish; but I already love her and cherish her."

But then, even as he thought, he realised what he must do. He must do more than feel love; he must give it and he must live it.

He took a Christmas card and, while his heart was full, began to write.

He knew not what unseen hand guided his, but this is what he wrote on that card and slipped under the Christmas tree with a small gift he had made her.

"My precious, precious one...

"This Christmas, though I have nothing, I will give you everything.

"I give you my promise to treat you always as a beautiful soul created by a loving God. I give you my word that I will protect you and care for you as I would a treasure. I give you my pledge to honour you as a person worthy of special honour.

"But most of all, I offer you the gift of love, all I have to give, now and always.

"Though I cannot give you worldly goods, I give you the greatest gift I can give. Though you have little, you will never again, not for one minute, want for love.

"From this day forth, with every word, every thought, every deed, this is how I shall try to live — for you.

"I am a simple man, but I know this of life... the greatest gift of all is the gift of love.

"And it is the greatest gift because it is the only gift that, when given away, grows — both in the person who receives and the person who gives. It is the gift that truly knows no bounds."

And so, boundless love surrounded that family on that Christmas morning and every day after. It was enough to carry them through the bad days and enough to make them soar on the good days, so that they never really felt poor again.

It was as the man had said ... it grew, and grew, and grew...

And the man never quite realised that he was already achieving his purpose in life. After all, there can hardly be a loftier goal in life than to drop seeds of love and nurture them and watch them grow.

All else simply follows.

■

What Christmas

Means

Through the

Years:

A Collection of

Thoughts and

Aspirations

for Christmas

Writers, presidents, and men and women from all walks of life have always been willing to speak out about Christmas, its true meaning, and the Christmas Spirit that grips us all at this time of the year. A snapshot of these thoughts and insights follow, but first, an old favourite.

More than 100 years ago, eight-year-old Virginia O'Hanlon wrote a letter to the editor of New York's *Sun newspaper,* and the paper responded quickly with an unsigned editorial on September 21, 1897.

The response was penned by a veteran newsman, Francis Pharcellus Church, and it has become history's most reprinted newspaper editorial, appearing in part or whole in dozens of languages in books, movies, other editorials, and on posters and stamps.

Virginia wrote: "Dear Editor, I am 8 years old. Some of my little friends say there is no Santa Claus. Papa says, 'If you see it in *The Sun,* it's so.' Please tell me the truth; is there a Santa Claus?"

And the response?

Yes, Virginia,
There is a Santa Claus

Virginia, your little friends are wrong. They have been affected by the scepticism of a sceptical age. They do not believe except they see. They think that nothing can be which is not comprehensible by their little minds.

All minds, Virginia, whether they be men's or children's are little. In this great universe of ours, man is a mere insect, an ant, in his intellect, as compared with the boundless world about him, as measured by the intelligence capable of grasping the whole of truth and knowledge.

Yes, Virginia, there is a Santa Claus. He exists as certainly as love and generosity and devotion exist, and you know that they abound and give to your life its highest beauty and joy.

Santa, as recorded by *The Sun* in 1897.

Alas! How dreary would be the world if there were no Santa Claus! It would be as dreary as if there were no Virginias.

There would be no child-like faith then, no poetry, no romance to make tolerable this existence.

We should have no enjoyment, except in sense and sight. The eternal light with which childhood fills the world would be extinguished.

Not believe in Santa Claus! You might as well not believe in fairies!

You might get your papa to hire men to watch in all the chimneys on Christmas eve to catch Santa Claus, but even if you did not see Santa Claus coming down, what would that prove? Nobody sees Santa Claus, but that is no sign that there is no Santa Claus.

The most real things in the world are those that neither children nor men can see.

Did you ever see fairies dancing on the lawn? Of course not, but that's no proof that they are not there.

Virginia O'Hanlon

Nobody can conceive or imagine all the wonders there are unseen and unseeable in the world. You tear apart the baby's rattle and see what makes the noise inside, but there is a veil covering the unseen world which not the strongest man, nor even the united strength of all the strongest men that ever lived, could tear apart.

Only faith, fancy, poetry, love, romance, can push aside that curtain and view and picture the supernal beauty and glory beyond.

Is it all real? Ah, Virginia, in all this world there is nothing else real and abiding.

No Santa Claus! Thank God! he lives, and he lives forever. A thousand years from now, Virginia, nay, ten times ten thousand years from now, he will continue to make glad the heart of childhood.

Francis Pharcellus Church

And now for how others have seen Christmas over the years:

"Are you willing to stoop down and consider the needs and desires of little children; to remember the weaknesses and loneliness of people who are growing old; to stop asking how much your friends love you, and to ask yourself if you love them enough; to bear in mind the things that other people have to bear on their hearts; to trim your lamp so that it will give more light and less smoke, and to carry it in front so that your shadow will fall behind you; to make a grave for your ugly thoughts and a garden for your kindly feelings, with the gate open? Are you willing to do these things for a day? Then you are ready to keep Christmas!"
~~ Henry van Dyke

"And how did little Tim behave?" asked Mrs Cratchit, when she had rallied Bob on his credulity and Bob had hugged his daughter to his heart's content.

"As good as gold," said Bob, "and better. Somehow he gets thoughtful, sitting by himself so much, and thinks the strangest things you ever heard. He told me, coming home, that he hoped the people saw him in the church, because he was a cripple, and it might be pleasant to them to remember upon Christmas Day, who made lame beggars walk, and blind men see."

~~ *Charles Dickens*, A Christmas Carol

"The human life cycle no less than evolves around the box; from the open-topped box called a bassinet, to the pine box we call a coffin, the box is our past and, just as assuredly, our future. It should not surprise us then that the lowly box plays such a significant role in the first Christmas story. For Christmas began in a humble, hay-filled box of splintered wood. The Magi, wise men who had travelled far to see the infant king, laid treasure-filled boxes at the feet of that holy child. And in the end, when He had ransomed our sins with His blood, the Lord of Christmas was laid down in a box of stone. How fitting that each Christmas season brightly wrapped boxes skirt the pine boughs of Christmas trees around the world. "

~ *Richard Paul Evans*, The Christmas Box

"I know what I really want for Christmas. I want my childhood back. Nobody is going to give me that. I might give at least the memory of it to myself if I try. I know it doesn't make sense, but since when is Christmas about sense, anyway? It is about a child, of long ago and far away, and it is about the child of now. In you and me. Waiting behind the door of, or hearts for, something wonderful to happen. A child who is impractical, unrealistic, simple-minded and terribly vulnerable to joy."

~~ *Robert Fulghum*, All I Really Need to Know I Learned in Kindergarten.

◊◊◊

"Let the children have their night of fun and laughter. Let the gifts of Father Christmas delight their play. Let us grown-ups share to the full in their unstinted pleasures before we turn again to the stern task and the formidable years that lie before us, resolved that, by our sacrifice and daring, these same children shall not be robbed of their inheritance or denied their right to live in a free and decent world."

~~ *Winston Churchill*,
Christmas Eve Message, 1941.

"Snowflakes swirl down gently in the deep blue haze beyond the window. The outside world is a dream. Inside, the fireplace is brightly lit, and the Yule log crackles with orange and crimson sparks. There's a steaming mug in your hands, warming your fingers. There's a friend seated across from you in the cosy chair, warming your heart. There is mystery unfolding."
~~ *Vera Nazarian,* The Perpetual Calendar of Inspiration.

"This Christmas mend a quarrel. Seek out a forgotten friend. Dismiss suspicion and replace it with trust. Write a letter. Give a soft answer. Encourage youth. Manifest your loyalty in word and deed. Keep a promise. Forgo a grudge. Forgive an enemy. Apologize. Try to understand. Examine your demands on others. Think first of someone else. Be kind. Be gentle. Laugh a little more. Express your gratitude. Welcome a stranger. Gladden the heart of a child. Take pleasure in the beauty and wonder of the earth. Speak your love, and then speak it again."
~~ *Howard W. Hunter*

"What is the spirit of Christmas, you ask? Let me give you the answer in a true story...

On a cold day in December, feeling especially warm in my heart for no other reason than it was the holiday season, I walked through the store sporting a big grin on my face. Though most people were far too busy going about their business to notice me, one elderly gentleman in a wheelchair brought his eyes up to meet mine as we neared each other traveling opposite directions. He slowed in passing just long enough to speak to me.

"Now that's a Christmas smile if I ever saw one," he said.

My lips stretched to their limit in response, and I thanked him for the compliment. Then we went our separate ways. But, as I thought about the man and how sweetly he'd touched me, I realized something simply wonderful! In that brief, passing interaction, we'd exchanged heart-felt gifts! And that, my friend, is the spirit of Christmas. "

~~ *Richelle E. Goodrich*

"Go back to that night when Divine Light, in order to illumine the darkness of men, tabernacled Himself in the world He had made… The angels and a star caught up in the reflection of that Light, as a torch lighted by a torch, and passed it on to the watchers of sheep and the searchers of skies. And lo! As the shepherds watched their flocks about the hills of Bethlehem, they were shaken by the light of the angels. And lo! As wise men from beyond the land of Media and Persia searched the heavens, the brilliance of a star, like a tabernacle lamp in the sanctuary of God's creation, beckoned them on to the stable, where the star seemed to lose its light in the unearthly brilliance of the Light of the Word."

~~ *Fulton J. Sheen*

"And the Grinch, with his Grinch-feet ice cold in the snow, stood puzzling and puzzling, how could it be so? It came without ribbons. It came without tags. It came without packages, boxes or bags. And he puzzled and puzzled 'till his puzzler was sore. Then the Grinch thought of something he hadn't before. What if Christmas, he thought, doesn't come from a store? What if Christmas, perhaps, means a little bit more?"

~~ *Dr. Seuss*

"I have always thought of Christmas time, when it has come round, as a good time; a kind, forgiving, charitable time; the only time I know of, in the long calendar of the year, when men and women seem by one consent to open their shut-up hearts freely, and to think of people below them as if they really were fellow passengers to the grave, and not another race of creatures bound on other journeys."

~~ *Charles Dickens,* A Christmas Carol

"Let us remember that the Christmas heart is a giving heart, a wide open heart that thinks of others first. The birth of the baby Jesus stands as the most significant event in all history, because it has meant the pouring into a sick world the healing medicine of love, which has transformed all manner of hearts for almost two thousand years. Underneath all those bulging bundles is this beating Christmas heart."

~~ *George Matthew Adams*, The Christmas Heart

"Off to one side sits a group of shepherds. They sit silently on the floor, perhaps perplexed, perhaps in awe, no doubt in amazement. Their night watch had been interrupted by an explosion of light from heaven and a symphony of angels. God goes to those who have time to hear him - and so, on this cloudless night, he went to simple shepherds."
~~ *Max Lucado*

◊◊◊

"Christmas waves a magic wand over this world, and behold, everything is softer and more beautiful."
~~ *Norman Vincent Peale*

"He who has not Christmas in his heart will never find it under a tree."
~~ *Roy L. Smith*

"I am not alone at all," I thought. "I was never alone at all. And that, of course, is the message of Christmas. We are never alone. Not when the night is darkest, the wind coldest, the world seemingly most indifferent. For this is still the time God chooses."

~~ *Taylor Caldwell*

◊◊◊

"The only real blind person at Christmas-time is he who has not Christmas in his heart."

~~ *Helen Keller*

◊◊◊

"It is Christmas every time you let God love others through you... yes, it is Christmas every time you smile at your brother and offer him your hand."

~~ *Mother Teresa*

"Christmas gift suggestions: To your enemy, forgiveness. To an opponent, tolerance. To a friend, your heart. To a customer, service. To all, charity. To every child, a good example. To yourself, respect."

~~ *Oren Arnold*

◊◊◊

"Unless we make Christmas an occasion to share our blessings, all the snow in Alaska won't make it 'white'."

~~ *Bing Crosby*

◊◊◊

"It comes every year and will go on forever. And along with Christmas belong the keepsakes and the customs. Those humble, everyday things a mother clings to, and ponders, like Mary, in the secret spaces of her heart."

~~ *Marjorie Holmes*

"What is Christmas? It is tenderness for the past, courage for the present, hope for the future. It is a fervent wish that every cup may overflow with blessings rich and eternal, and that every path may lead to peace."
~~ Agnes M. Pahro

"I truly believe that if we keep telling the Christmas story, singing the Christmas songs, and living the Christmas spirit, we can bring joy and happiness and peace to this world."
~~ Norman Vincent Peale

Christmas - that magic blanket that wraps itself about us, that something so intangible that it is like a fragrance. It may weave a spell of nostalgia. Christmas may be a day of feasting, or of prayer, but always it will be a day of remembrance - a day in which we think of everything we have ever loved."
~~ Augusta E. Rundell

Whatever else be lost among the years,
Let us keep Christmas still a shining thing:
Whatever doubts assail us, or what fears,
Let us hold close one day, remembering
Its poignant meaning for the hearts of men.
Let us get back our childlike faith again.

~~ *Grace Noll Crowell*

'Twas the night before Christmas, when all through the house
Not a creature was stirring — not even a mouse:
The stockings were hung by the chimney with care,
In hopes that St. Nicholas soon would be there.

~~ Clement C. Moore

Somehow not only for Christmas
But all the long year through,
The joy that you give to others
Is the joy that comes back to you.
And the more you spend in blessing
The poor and lonely and sad,
The more of your heart's possessing
Returns to make you glad.

~~ *John Greenleaf Whittier*

Silent Night:

The True Story of a

Christmas Miracle

Brian Morgan

Once upon a time,

long, long ago...

When stories start off like this, you always wonder whether they are true or not. Well, this one is true, although, when old stories are lost over time and then slowly found again, little by little, the truth is sometimes hard to find.

And when people change the story for one reason or another, or add their own twist to it, the truth becomes very elusive indeed.

For example, some people say this story started in the village of Hallein, in the Austrian Alps, but that is where *part* of the story *ended*, as we shall see. It started in Austria, certainly, but *not* in Hallein.

Most people agree that the story started in the village of Oberndorf, near Salzburg. Hmm, not quite true, but that is where we shall start our journey that will eventually take us around the world.

It was a white Christmas.

Most also agree *when* the story started - Christmas Eve, 24th December 1818 - nearly 200 years ago, in the modest Church of St Nicholas at Oberndorf.

Well, even these things are not strictly true, but we'll stay with Christmas Eve, 1818, in Oberndorf, for a moment.

I'm sorry if I sound a little mysterious, but this whole story was a mystery for so long, only becoming clearer with an important discovery just a few short years ago.

And I'm sure you'll forgive me if I've had to read a little between the lines to be able to relate a story that is true in its essence.

Now, in that part of the world, Austria, it was, as always, a white Christmas.

Snow was falling gently in soft drifts to cover the wooden and stone houses in Oberndorf with a white blanket.

People had cut down young spruce trees and the children had decorated them with candles, and with fruit and nuts, as was the custom.

And so, the holiest of nights drew near, and despite the chatter of the children, a peaceful hush fell over the village.

Soon the bells would peal from the little Church of St Nicholas to announce Midnight Mass, and people would tramp and sleigh through the snow to celebrate the birth of Jesus with prayer and song.

The children were excited: it was the one day of the year when they were allowed to stay up until midnight.

However, unknown to the preoccupied people of the village, something was amiss in the church.

Something was very wrong indeed.

They had cut down young spruce trees.

Father Joseph Mohr
as a young man.

The curate, Father Joseph Mohr, was a devout young man of 26, who had been a priest for less than three years and had only been appointed Assistant Priest at the Church of St Nicholas one year before.

And now he was desperately unhappy.

Father Joseph was a man who loved music. In fact, it was his natural flair for music, they say, that led to him becoming a priest.

Born into poverty as the son of a seamstress and a soldier, he earned money as a boy by singing and by playing his guitar and a violin in public.

His earnings from music allowed him to survive through school and university, where his talent caught the eye of a priest, who persuaded him to join the clergy.

And then, when he did become a priest, he sometimes surprised his congregation by strumming his guitar and singing folk songs and hymns.

He just loved music.

Imagine then, his distress, on the morning of Christmas Eve, to find the church organ out of order.

No matter how hard he pumped those pedals, all he could squeeze out of it was a wheeze like a rusty gate.

Some say mice had eaten holes in the organ's bellows. Some have tried to imagine other things wrong with it, but, whatever the problem, Father Joseph would not be able to get it fixed in time for Christmas Mass.

That much was certain.

Christmas Eve without music was unthinkable. What to do? What to do? Carols without the organ just didn't seem right.

Then, as he prepared the church for Mass and worried himself sick over the music, the miracle started.

And, as miracles sometimes do, it started with just a spark of an idea.

A very simple idea.

All he could squeeze out of it was a wheeze like a rusty gate.

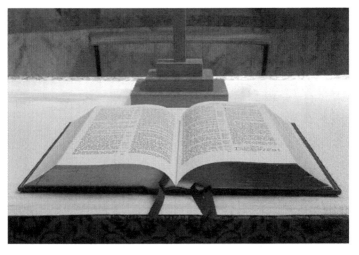

"Unto you is born this day, in the City of David, a saviour..."

His mind went back to his first Christmas as a priest. Back, in fact, to the *real* start of this story - Christmas Eve, 1816, two years earlier, in the village of Mariapfarr.

He had been sitting at his desk in his study there, reading the Bible and preparing his Christmas sermon.

He had just read the words: "Unto you is born this day, in the City of David, a saviour...", when there was a knock at his door.

He opened it, to find a peasant woman, shivering in the cold. She had come to tell him of a poor charcoal-maker's wife, who had given birth earlier that morning.

The lady believed that the blessing of a priest was vital for new life to flourish.

"Could you not come to bless the infant, so that it might live and thrive?" she asked him.

In her arms, the baby slept peacefully.
Safe, serene, a scene to melt the heart.

The young priest was jolted out of his thoughts. A baby born... at Christmas?

The snow was heavy and the cold seeped into his very bones through his old, worn coat, but he just had to go, though time was short.

And he was so glad he did, because what he found moved him as nothing had since his ordination.

In a small cabin, old but well-kept, a single lamp and a log fire lit a scene of beauty and calm.

His eyes barely took in the simple, homely elegance before they found the young mother sitting up on a rough-hewn bed, smiling with joy that he had come.

In her arms, the baby slept peacefully. Safe, serene, a scene to melt the heart. Mother and child, the age-old bond that had delighted mankind for millennia.

The room did not resemble a stable in the City of David, Bethlehem, but, in every other way, the sight of the mother and child - and that beautiful smell only a new-born baby has - took his thoughts back to a manger so very long ago.

With trembling hands, he blessed mother and infant and, as he did so, bells in the distance announced Midnight Mass.

So he made his farewell and hurried back to the church, though he could think of nothing else but the scene he had just witnessed.

For young Father Joseph, it was his own personal Christmas gift - one he would treasure for the rest of his days.

For days and weeks afterwards, his thoughts kept returning to the village baby and the one born nearly two thousand years earlier.

His grandfather lived within a short stroll, and the two men often discussed the miracle of birth and new life, and they certainly discussed this baby.

Finally, the scholarly priest decided he had to write of his experience and how it had shaped his vision of the birth of Jesus.

His words seemed to form themselves into verse, and, as with all good writing, his quill seemed to be guided by an unseen hand; his words inspired by the beauty of what he felt.

The Father Joseph Mohr
Chapel in Austria.

His quill seemed to be guided by an unseen hand.

The poem did not have a name, but its opening line was to touch hearts wherever it was heard in its original German language:

Stille Nacht,

Heilige Nacht.

Or, in English:

Silent Night,

Holy Night.

When Father Joseph had finished his six stanzas, he himself was surprised at their beauty and simplicity and his heart was full.

He packed the poem away safely with his few possessions, and it's a good thing for us and for the world that he did so, because soon afterwards he became ill and was sent to Salzburg, with all those possessions, to recuperate.

After he did regain his health and his strength, he was appointed curate at the Church of St Nicholas, Oberndorf.

And this is where we left him, remember, on Christmas Eve 1818, feeling the first tiny spark of a miracle that might solve his distress over a stubborn organ that refused to work.

The opening words of his verse, *Silent Night, Holy Night*, had suddenly slipped out of the recesses of his memory and now began to repeat themselves, over and over, in his mind:

The famous guitar is still a big
attraction in its museum case
in Austria.

Excited, he quickly found the verse he had written two years earlier. He read it again and the same feeling of peace and joy filled his heart once more.

If only he had thought about setting it to music earlier, for music is what was needed now. A poem was just not enough.

Surely it was now too late, with less than 12 hours before Mass?

He tried to pluck out a tune on his guitar, but it was no use. He was too frantic, and he could not find the music worthy of the words.

Then another little part of the miracle fell into place. He remembered his friend, Franz.

Franz Xaver Gruber was 31 and was the school teacher at Arnsdorf, only 20 minutes away on foot.

"Yes, Franz," thought the priest, "He is a much better composer than I am. If anyone can do it, he can. He just loves a challenge."

As Father Joseph hurried over to Arnsdorf, he thought of his friend and his love of music.

Franz, as a child, had had to hide his feelings about music. His father was a hard-working weaver, and very strict. He could not see how music could be suitable work that would earn money for his son's future family.

The old school and Gruber residence is now an Austrian tourist attraction.

But Franz loved music so much, he did something he felt ashamed of - he crept out of the house at night to take music lessons from the local school master.

Fortunately, it all came to a happy ending, when Mr Gruber heard his son playing the organ.

He was so overwhelmed, he forgave his son and allowed him to continue his study of music.

Franz became a teacher himself because teachers were expected to serve as organist and choir master at the local church.

When he was sent to Arnsdorf to teach, he had been welcomed at the Church of St Nicholas in the neighbouring village, where he played the organ and became choir master.

So, Father Joseph rushed to see Franz and his wife, Elizabeth, and their children, in their quarters above the school.

He gushed out his dilemma and thrust his verse into Franz Gruber's hands.

Vikar
Josef Mohr
1792 – 1848
schuf den Text des Liedes
in Oberndorf

Lehrer
Franz X. Gruber
1787 – 1863
die Melodie
in Arnsdorf

An artist's impression of the two men who gave
the world its favourite Christmas carol.

"Franz," he said, "can you compose a tune for these words? Perhaps suitable for a guitar, two voices - yours and mine - and a chorus?"

He hesitated.

"And can you do it in time for Midnight Mass tonight?"

Franz read the words and was struck by their innocence and charm.

"My friend," he said, "what you ask is impossible, and yet... how can I not try? I'm sure we don't need an organ to be heard by the good Lord."

He wasted no more words, but went straight to his piano and began to search for notes as he kept repeating the words, searching for a rhythm he could use.

Father Joseph saw that he could do no more, and hurried back to the church to continue preparations.

Now, I don't know much about music, but I'm told that Franz Gruber used three of the most basic harmonies in the musical repertoire to create the now-famous melody for Father Joseph's verse.

He rushed to the church with his composition, with barely enough time for a hurried rehearsal before the bells began to peal to announce Midnight Mass.

Perhaps once in a lifetime, a special, magical night can touch the heart and stir the soul like no other - and, for the priest and the school teacher and the villagers of Oberndorf, this was such a night.

The snow had stopped, but had covered everything with its white beauty. The stars were as bright in the sky as they must have been over the stable at Bethlehem.

And out of the houses and down the hills and along the valleys, people carrying rush torches converged on the Church of St Nicholas in a procession of whispering, flickering light.

The stage was surely set for a miracle.

People were converging on the Church of St Nicholas.
The stage was set for a miracle.

However, the villagers were used to organ music as they entered the church, and were mystified by the silence that greeted them.

They watched Father Joseph slowly climb into the pulpit. He seemed a little nervous and embarrassed.

"My dear people," he said, hesitantly, "I have some disappointing news this Christmas... our church organ is broken... we can coax no music from it, try as we may."

He held his hand up as the people murmured.

"However, our choir-master, Franz Gruber, and I have something we would like to try for you, if you will allow us.'

He motioned for Franz to join him at the front of the church and for the choir to rise.

And the next few minutes changed Christmas forever.

The choir members rose to their feet and Christmas
was changed forever.

As Father Joseph strummed his guitar, his fine tenor voice was joined by Franz Gruber's deep bass to create perhaps the most beautiful harmony and the most heart-felt song to ever fill the rafters of that little church.

On each refrain, the choir joined in, and the people sat, hushed and absorbed in the soft, yet soaring sounds that must have brought to mind the glorious sounds of angels on high.

And this is what they sang:

Silent Night, Holy Night,

All is calm, all is bright.

'Round yon virgin Mother and Child,

Holy infant so tender and mild,

Sleep in heavenly peace,

Sleep in heavenly peace.

Silent Night, Holy Night,

Shepherds quake at the sight.

Glories stream from heaven afar,

Heav'nly hosts sing Alleluia;

Christ the Saviour is born,

Christ the Saviour is born.

Silent Night, Holy Night,

Son of God, love's pure light.

Radiant beams from Thy holy face,

With the dawn of redeeming grace,

Jesus, Lord, at Thy birth,

Jesus, Lord, at Thy birth.

The villagers sat in the narrow pews, awed by the simplicity and the innocence of the words and music. No music on Christmas Eve?

This was music as they had never heard before and their hearts were full as they heard Father Joseph celebrate Mass for a Christmas they would never forget.

Father Joseph and his friend Franz Gruber had pulled off something of a miracle - and that is where it might have all ended.

The song was not heard again for a few years, but that Christmas Eve was just the start of the miracle.

Just the start...

The old church organ continued to be contrary and an organ builder and repairman called Karl Mauracher was back and forth to fix it - and he became part of the miracle.

In 1825, he finally rebuilt the organ, but, while in the loft, he came across the words and music of *Silent Night*.

Father Joseph had moved from that parish by then, but Franz Gruber was delighted for Karl Mauracher to share the song with others, so the organ master showed it to troupes of travelling Tyrolean singers (much like the Trapp Family Singers of *Sound of Music* fame).

He had no idea what a great treasure he was passing from two unknown composers to the entire world.

Of course, the miracle might also have ended right there, but everyone who heard this song was enchanted by it, and wanted to sing it.

Families like the Strassers and the Rainers began singing what they thought was a simple folk song they called *Song from Heaven*. Audiences were enthralled.

The next to be part of the miracle were four little angels of the Strasser family, called Caroline, Joseph, Andrea and tiny Amalie (or "Maly"). Among other places, they performed *Song from Heaven* at a concert at the Leipzig Fair at Christmas in 1832. Leipzig was in the Kingdom of Saxony, Germany.

It was the children's task to attract the crowds with their singing at such events so their parents could sell gloves to people. And attract the crowds they did, especially with their folk song, called *Song from Heaven*.

"Those Strassers," people would say, "sing like nightingales."

About this time, a publisher printed the song for the first time. He simply called it a folk song - and the names of Father Joseph and Franz Gruber were nowhere to be seen.

One day, the children sang and were approached by an elderly gentleman called Mr Pohlenz, who was the General Director of Music for the Kingdom of Saxony. They were thrilled when he gave them tickets to one of the concerts he conducted in Leipzig. Another little piece of the miracle was falling into place.

At the end of the concert, they were shocked when Mr Pohlenz rose to address the audience - the ladies in their colourful, rustling gowns and the gentlemen in their top hats - and the King and Queen of Saxony, who were present.

"There are four children here," the concert master announced, "with the most beautiful voices I have heard in many a year.

"Perhaps they might be persuaded to sing for their Royal Majesties."

The children were stunned, but how could they refuse?

Little Maly led them to the stage and, as a hush fell over the audience, they began to sing.

Their first song was *Song from Heaven*, and, when they finished, there were long moments of almost reverend silence - and then the king and queen led the standing ovation of wild applause.

Their first song was the "folksong" they called
Song from Heaven.

The king and queen were so impressed that the queen asked the children to come to the castle to sing for her children at Christmas. And so it was that, on Christmas Eve 1832, in the Royal Saxon Court Chapel in Plessenburg Castle, the Strasser children sang at the end of Christmas services:

Silent Night, Holy Night,

All is calm, all is bright...

And the song, composed by two unknown men and sung by little children, reached the ears of royalty and began its journey around the world.

The song then crossed the Atlantic Ocean with the next piece of the miracle - the Rainer family. They had already sung the carol before an audience that included Emperor Franz, of Austria, and Tzar Alexander, of Russia. Then, in 1839, they performed *Stille Nacht* for the first time across the seas in New York, America.

This was the first time English-speaking people had heard the song and it seemed to them as pure and fresh as an Alpine stream.

King Frederick

The names Father Joseph Mohr and Franz Gruber were unknown, and the two men had no idea of the reaction their composition was generating.

People were so impressed by the song and the music that they began to speculate that a famous composer, like Haydn, Mozart or Beethoven had created it.

Year by year, the carol became more and more popular.

In Prussia, King Frederick William IV ordered the Royal Cathedral Choir to sing it for him every Christmas.

Father Joseph, sadly, died as he had lived, penniless, in 1848, struck down by pneumonia.

He never found out that his verse had reached some of the far corners of the earth.

His final resting place is a tiny Alpine ski resort called Wagrain, where he had spent his last days as pastor of the church.

True to his lifestyle, he had given all his earnings to the old people of the village and to help educate the children.

The local school is still called the Joseph Mohr School in his honour.

A report to the bishop described him as "a reliable friend of mankind and a gentle, loving father to the poor."

Father Joseph -

"Loving father to the poor."

Franz Gruber only heard of the song's success in 1854, 36 years after he had composed the tune, when King Frederick William began searching for the source of the carol.

Franz sent a letter to the king telling how the song started.

For a long time, few could believe that two such humble men could create a Christmas carol that had endeared itself to the world.

Late in Franz Gruber's life, he and his family had moved to Hallein - remember Hallein? There Franz died in 1863, at the age of 67.

During his lifetime, he had produced a number of arrangements of his composition, five of which still exist.

But, when he died, few believed he had composed the music, and fewer still believed Father Joseph had written the words.

In the year Franz died, the Reverend John Freeman Young (later Bishop Young) translated Joseph Mohr's six stanzas in German into the three stanzas in English we sing today.

The long-lost arrangement of the carol, in Father Joseph's
own handwriting, discovered as late as 1995.

The controversy over authorship of the carol was finally put to rest when a long-lost arrangement of the carol, in Father Joseph's own hand-writing, was discovered as late as 1995, just a few years ago and 179 years after he wrote his poem.

It was found to be authentic by handwriting experts and historians, and has now been proclaimed as the earliest known manuscript of *Silent Night*.

And, in the upper right corner, Father Joseph had written: "Melody by Fr. Xav. Gruber", ensuring his friend's fame.

That manuscript, together with other marvellous exhibits, including Father Joseph's guitar, is on display in the Franz Gruber Museum, in the former Gruber home in Hallein. One of the exhibits is an account, by Franz himself, of how the carol was created. His grave is outside the museum and villagers decorate it every year with a Christmas tree.

Everyone now knows the authors of the carol that has been called "the musical symbol of Christmas" and, by Austrians, "the song heard around the world."

And indeed it is heard around the world.

The song has worked its way into the hearts of people on every continent on earth, in every town and city where there is a Christmas.

It has been translated into more than 300 languages and is heard and sung by countless millions every Christmas "from small chapels in the Andes to great cathedrals in Antwerp and Rome".

St Peter's Basilica in Rome.

Such is the miracle of *Silent Night*, and so many people have played their part: a priest, a teacher, an organ master, little children, folk singers, kings and queens - and the millions upon millions of people throughout the world who have taken this simply tune and elegant words into their hearts.

Many, many singers, including Bing Crosby and Elvis Presley, just had to have this carol in their repertoire.

This year I heard it sung in Japanese by a group of children called the Little Angels of Nagasaki, and, if this is what the Strasser children sounded like, then they truly did sound like nightingales.

But that is not the end of the story: that is not the end of the miracle.

Down through the generations, all over the world, *Silent Night* has shown a miraculous power to create feelings of heavenly peace, even in times of war and horror.

The First World War was supposed to be "the war to end all wars". It was not, unfortunately, and, in many ways, it was the worst war ever fought. Millions died and there was savage hand-to-hand combat in muddy, gas-filled trenches.

On Christmas Eve, 1914, in the middle of this savage fighting between Germans and Allies, including Australians, the opponents held an uneasy truce, a cease-fire, because it was the holiest day of the year. No-one was sure if the truce, on what was called the Western Front, would be broken at any moment.

Suddenly, in the still of the night, a lone voice came from the German trenches and was heard across "no-man's land", the space between the lines of trenches:

Stille Nacht,

Heilige Nacht...

Other German voices joined in, hesitantly, then gradually louder to sing the carol of heavenly peace.

Across no-man's land, the Allies, including my fellow Australians, were mystified, but then slowly joined in, singing in English.

For a few quiet moments in a horrible, horrible war, heavenly peace descended as rough voices in German and English blended in song.

Fierce opponents approached each other, shook hands, and even found a small Christmas tree. It was a moment never to be forgotten.

At the same time, far away in a prison camp in Siberia, Russia, German, Hungarian and Austrian prisoners of war broke into a chorus of *Silent Night*, each in his own language.

The Russian commandant of the prison had tears in his eyes.

"This is the first time in more than a year of war," he is quoted as saying, "that I have been able to forget that you and I are supposed to be enemies."

The miracle was at work again.

In the Second World War, in Czechoslovakia in 1944, German Nazis had overrun the country.

A German officer, visiting an orphanage, asked if any children there knew how to sing *Silent Night* in German. A boy and a girl began to sing, nervously, then suddenly stopped.

They realised that, in that part of the country, mostly Jews knew German, and the Germans had been killing Jews. The children were terrified.

But the German officer just smiled.

"Don't be afraid," he said. He, too, had been touched by the miracle of *Silent Night*.

On Christmas Eve, in 1951, during the Korean War, a young American soldier called John Thorsness was on guard duty when he was startled by a noise.

He was sure it was the enemy creeping up on him in the dark.

His finger was on the trigger of his gun, when a small group of Koreans emerged slowly from the darkness.

They were hesitant, but smiling. As he stood and watched, the group sang *Silent Night* in Korean, just for him, then slipped back into the darkness.

The miracle continued for one awe-struck, lonely soldier.

Over the years, in war zones, in prisons, in hospitals, in refugee camps, in the most distressful of circumstances, someone, somewhere, will begin to sing *Silent Night*, and the miracle of heavenly peace will touch hearts and slip into troubled souls.

No-one really knows why *Silent Night* became probably our most beloved carol or hymn for Christmas. Perhaps it was the tender, gentle words that evoke feelings of the birth in a manger so very long ago. Perhaps it is the peaceful, easy-to-remember tune that plucks at the heart-strings.

There are many parts to the miracle of *Silent Night*. The words flowed from the heart of a quiet, modest priest. The music was composed by a young teacher unknown outside his tiny corner of the world.

These days there would be a celebrity to sing the song at its world premiere. In yester-year, only the voices of the priest and the teacher - tenor and bass - blended to create a masterpiece of world music.

And this masterpiece - this miracle - of heavenly peace has crossed all barriers of language, culture and border to conquer hearts everywhere.

Just as it conquers yours every Christmas, and will again this year, for the *Song from Heaven* will surely ring out for all time for people of good will.

The miracle of this carol is still a miracle and will continue as long as there are voices to sing and hearts to feel the message that "glories stream from heaven afar".

It does not matter that the interval of heavenly peace felt by those who hear *Silent Night* might only be short.

In a world all too full of hatred and war, a short blessing is a blessing still - and surely a miraculous gift every Christmas. ∎

When the song of the angel is stilled,
When the star in the sky is gone,
When the kings and princes are home,
When the shepherds are back with their flock,
The work of Christmas begins:
To find the lost — To heal the broken —
To feed the hungry —
To release the prisoner —
To rebuild the nations —
To bring peace among brothers and sisters —
To make music in the heart.

Howard Thurman

A Word from the Author

If you liked this book, could I ask you to do something for me to help me promote it? It cannot be found in bookstores, but can be found at Amazon, Smashwords and other eBook online stores.

But, since it's not in bricks and mortar stores, I have to find ways to let people know about it.

If you could help me in this task, you might provide a helpful service for future readers.

One of the best ways to promote books these days is to return to Amazon (to the page where the book is listed) and post a comment or review or just a few words that might help people decide whether to buy it or not.

Any mention in social networks or book clubs and so on is also very helpful.

I think you know more than I do about spreading the word to friends, and I'm sure you'd be more comfortable talking about my book than I am.

If it helps, I'm hoping to offer signed copies of my books with your personal message on books bought as gifts for others. Details will be posted on www.brianmorganbooks.com.

On that site you'll also find reviews and testimonials, and details of my other books and of the many completed books in the queue waiting for publication.

I hope you get the opportunity to enjoy and benefit from my other books as time goes by.

Thank you, and may we meet again,

Brian

PS. I would also like to hear from readers any thoughts or advice or comments you may have. I'd also like to hear your Christmas stories for possible future editions. Why not contact me through the website, or at brianmorganbooks@gmail.com.

About the Author

Brian Morgan is an award-winning, best-selling writer, who is dedicating the senior years of his life to inspiring and motivating people through his books and other writings.

He has been a business and thought leader, a business founder, a national award-winning journalist, editor and publisher, and an internationally acclaimed author.

He has also been honoured by his community on numerous occasions for his long service to various community groups and organisations.

More can be read about him on various Internet platforms and on his own website at www.brianmorganbooks.com.

In 2012, in association with The Writers Trust, he started a program to publish all of his books in print and as eBooks. All the details can best be found on the website.

Brian's new mission in life is summed up in his site's logo: Stories to Touch Lives.